THE BUFFALO
AND THE INDIANS

A Shared Destiny

DOROTHY HINSHAW PATENT   Photographs by WILLIAM MUÑOZ

CLARION BOOKS / *New York*

Clarion Books
a Houghton Mifflin Company imprint
215 Park Avenue South, New York, NY 10003
Text copyright © 2006 by Dorothy Hinshaw Patent
Photographs copyright © 2006 by William Muñoz

The text was set in 15-point Slimbach.

www.houghtonmifflinbooks.com

Manufactured in China.

Library of Congress Cataloging-in-Publication Data

Patent, Dorothy Hinshaw.
The buffalo and the Indians : a shared destiny / by Dorothy Hinshaw Patent ; photos by William Muñoz.
p. cm.
Includes bibliographical references and index.
ISBN-13: 978-0-618-48570-3
ISBN-10: 0-618-48570-8
1. American bison—Juvenile literature. 2. Indians of North America—Hunting—Juvenile literature.
3. Indians of North America—Food—Juvenile literature. 4. Indians of North America—
History—Juvenile literature. I. Muñoz, William, ill. II. Title.
E98.B8P37 2006
978.004'97—dc22   2005031744

SCP 10 9 8 7 6 5 4 3 2

FOR AMERICA'S FIRST PEOPLE

Contents

ACKNOWLEDGMENTS

Many people gave generously of their time to help us with this project, including Richard Clow, Pete Hale, Bob and Laura Hanson, Dave and Val Heider, Marilyn Hudson, Valentina LaPier, Jerry Lunak, Beth O'Rourke, Robert Pickering, Vicki Privett, Kate Shanley, and Curly Bear Wagner. Thanks also to the C.M. Russell Museum and its Buffalo Hunt Project, and to Joe Halko, sculptor of the buffalo cast for Valentina LaPier's *Iini Pikuni*.

Author's Note

For thousands of years, the Indian tribes that lived on the North American prairies depended on the buffalo for their survival. The people regarded this abundant, powerful animal as another tribe, one that was closely related to them, and they treated it with great respect and admiration. In this book, I trace the history of this relationship, from its beginnings in prehistory to the present.

Although the Plains Indian tribes had no written language, they communicated with stories, which they passed on from generation to generation. These stories often help explain tribal history or the origins of tribal customs, and they continue to have meaning today. Each chapter of this book begins with an Indian story that relates to the events described in the chapter. The stories have been selected from a number of different Plains Indian tribes to give a glimpse of their world views and story traditions. Bill Muñoz, photographer for the book, has created a photo collage for the beginning of each chapter.

"We are praying that mankind does wake up and think about the future, for we haven't just inherited this earth from our ancestors, we are borrowing it from our unborn children."

—Joseph Chasing Horse

Chapter One

ARRIVAL IN AMERICA

In the days of the grandfathers, buffalo lived under the earth. In the olden times, a story from the Teton tribe says, a man who was journeying came to a hill where there were many holes in the ground. He entered one of them. Inside, he found buffalo chips and buffalo tracks everywhere. He also found buffalo hairs where the buffalo had rubbed against the walls. These were the real buffalo, and they lived under the ground. Afterward, some of them came to the surface of the earth to live. Then the herds on the earth increased.

For hundreds of generations, Indians hunted the buffalo, also called the American bison, across the heartland of North America. This long relationship led to a deep feeling of kinship and dependency, one so close that some Indian stories say that people were once bison, or that bison were once people.

Several species of bison lived at different times in North America. The steppe bison (*Bison priscus*), which also lived in Europe, showed up first, at least 129,000 years ago. European Ice Age hunters pursued them and painted their images on cave walls. In 1979, a gold miner found the mummy of a steppe bison bull that died about 36,000 years ago north of what is now Fairbanks, Alaska. By studying this mummy, scientists have learned a lot about the steppe bison, which disappeared from most of North America about 12,000 years ago.

A truly giant bison (*Bison latifrons*), with horns measuring 9 feet (2.7 meters) from tip to tip, appears to have evolved from the steppe bison tens of thousands of years ago. It survived until perhaps 21,000 years ago. These huge animals lived at a time of mild climate, when giant ground sloths and the early ancestors of horses roamed a moist landscape of trees and grasslands in North America.

Another kind of bison lived in North America from about 71,000 years ago until 10,000 years ago. These animals were bigger than the American bison of today, with horns close to 3 feet (almost 1 meter) from tip to tip. Early Indian people seem to have hunted these antique bison (*Bison antiquus*) one or two at a time, using hand-held spears with big sturdy

A copy of a skull of the extinct giant bison, which lived in North America thousands of years ago. THREE AFFILIATED TRIBES MUSEUM.

points. By 8,500 years ago, hunters had discovered they could successfully pursue a different, smaller bison species by startling them into stampeding over a precipice into a gully below. There the hunters could harvest plenty of meat. This was the beginning of a hunting technique the Indians refined and used for thousands of years to come.

Living on the Prairie

In prehistoric times, grasslands covered the middle of North America, from the Rocky Mountains in the west to the forests of the east, and from southern Canada southward into northern Mexico. Giant elephant-like mammoths, ground sloths

Grasslands like this covered the heart of North America for tens of thousands of years.

weighing hundreds of pounds, camels, and many other remarkable creatures lived on the prairies along with the bison, allowing the people plenty of choice in their food. Then, about 10,000 years ago, most of these large animals became extinct. No one knows why they disappeared. Some scientists say they couldn't survive the climate changes occurring around that time, but others say the early people, called Paleoindians, hunted them to extinction. The modern American bison (*Bison bison*), however, survived and flourished. Whatever the reason for the disappearance of so much potential food, it forced the people from then on to rely mainly on the abundant bison for survival. The fate of the bison and the fate of the Indians became closely intertwined.

What Are Bison?

The American bison is a close relative of cattle. Scientists prefer the name "bison" to "buffalo" in order to avoid confusion with animals like the Asian water buffalo, which is only distantly related to bison. Both names are used, however, and traditionally the Indians have used the word "buffalo." Like cattle, bison live in herds. Two variations of the American bison exist: the wood bison of the north, once found only in Canada, and the plains bison, which lived in southern Canada and in the United States.

Bison are big, powerful animals. A mature bull can stand 6 feet (1.75 meters) tall at the shoulder and weigh more than a ton, while a cow weighs about half as much. Both cows

Pronghorn are one of the few large prairie animals to survive into modern times.

An American bison bull.

and bulls have a noticeable hump on their shoulders. Muscles in the hump make the neck strong, enabling the animal to use its head to push aside snow in the winter to get at the grass underneath. All bison have horns, but the bull's horns are bigger. In spite of their size and power, bison can run as fast as a horse. They can wheel about in an instant on their slim hind legs.

The hair over the back part of the body is dark brown, while the front part of the body is covered by a coat of lighter brown fur. Thick fur also covers the head, with especially dense, woolly hair on the forehead of the male. Both cows and bulls have beards. The bull's beard continues to get longer and thicker over the years, while the cow's beard stops growing when she is just a few years old.

A bison bull, cow, and calf. Note the large muscular humps on their shoulders.

The Buffalo's Year

The life of the plains bison is closely related to the seasons. Calves are born in the spring, when fresh, nutritious grasses grow on the prairies. At this time, the younger bison and the cows live together in herds, while the mature bulls live away from them, either by themselves or in their own smaller herds. The cinnamon-colored calves weigh thirty to forty pounds at birth and can stand up soon after.

At first, the calves feed only on their mothers' rich milk, but before long they begin nibbling bits of grass. The cows are very protective of the young ones, and they sometimes take turns babysitting for each other. During the summer, the

Bison cows take good care of their calves, which grow quickly on a diet of their mothers' milk.

Two bulls battle to see which is stronger.

calves romp and play together. As they grow, their humps and horns start developing. Their coats gradually turn darker, until the calves are the same chocolate brown as their mothers. When a herd moves to water or to a new pasture, the mature cows, which know the land well, lead the way.

The breeding season begins in late summer. The separate herds of cows and calves join to form larger herds, and mature bulls join them. Bulls challenge one another for the right to mate with the cows. If one of the bulls is clearly bigger and stronger, the smaller bull turns away. If they are well matched, they may fight, battling to see which is stronger. They face each other head on, pawing at the ground and bellowing with deep, rumbling voices. They butt their heads together and push, each trying to make the other give way.

The extra-thick fur on their foreheads helps cushion the blows. When the battle is over, the winning bull enters the herd of cows to choose his mate.

As winter approaches, bison grow longer, thicker coats. During a cold and windy winter, the bison herds move away

Note the dense fur on the bull's forehead.

In the winter, buffalo push the snow aside to get at the grass below.

from the open prairie, preferring the more protected woods along the rivers, where there is less wind and snow.

Indians on the Prairie

Scientists argue about how and when people came to live in North America. More than a hundred tribes eventually

This painting by George Catlin, done in the 1830s, shows a band of Sioux Indians moving camp. NATIONAL MUSEUM OF AMERICAN ART, SMITHSONIAN INSTITUTION.

inhabited the vast prairies, and each Indian tribe has an origin story describing how their people arrived upon the land.

Indians living on the Plains survived largely by hunting big game. Tribes that lived along rivers, such as the Mandan and Hidatsa, also grew crops of corn, beans, and squash. Farming people in the eastern plains, where water was relatively abundant, spent most of the year living in permanent villages. The hunting tribes of the north and west lived in small family groups called bands. The bands of a particular tribe would gather together for important occasions, such as for the Sun Dance in early summer.

The family bands moved their camps often and lived in tepees, which could be taken down and put back up easily. A tepee is made by placing long poles in a circle, leaning inward and tied together at the top. The poles support a covering made of buffalo hides sewn together. A tepee can be set up or taken down by a woman in an hour.

The Indians had no wheeled vehicles, and dogs were the Plains tribes' only animal companions. To move goods from place to place, two slim poles forming a *V* were bound together at one end, forming a travois, or sled. Smaller pieces of wood or a woven net were attached between the framing poles to carry the load. A dog was harnessed at the joined ends, and the tips of the poles dragged on the ground as the animal pulled the travois.

The early Indians first used spears for hunting. As time went on, they invented a tool called the atlatl, a throwing stick that hooked into the end of the spear shaft and allowed the hunter to throw the spear with much more power. Later people brought bows and arrows, which were quickly adopted by other groups. A hunter had to stand up to throw a spear, but he could crouch and hide behind a rock or tree while using a bow and arrows. He could then fire one arrow after another rapidly. Arrows were also more accurate than spears. While bison were the most abundant prey, early Indians also hunted deer, rabbits, sheep, bears, badgers, coyotes, and wood rats. In addition, they gathered a great variety of plants, especially fruits, berries, roots, and bulbs. But the buffalo was the mainstay of their diet.

Chapter Two

DEPENDING ON THE BUFFALO

The Blackfeet tell of how Old Man traveled over the earth, creating people and rivers and grass. When he reached a northerly river, he gathered up some mud and shaped it into images of people. After he breathed upon the images, they came to life and asked, "What shall we eat?" So Old Man took up more mud and made it into the shapes of buffalo, and he breathed upon them and they began to run. He told the people that the buffalo would be their food, but they didn't know how to hunt.

So Old Man took them high atop a cliff and showed them how to make a large V by marking the borders with piles of rock. "Hide behind these rocks," he said. "I will drive the buffalo toward you," and he did. When the buffalo reached the opening of the V, the people rose up, keeping the animals inside it. When the buffalo ran over the cliff and fell to their death below, Old Man showed the people how to use sharp rocks to cut the meat, how to make a tepee with the skins, and how to kill those animals that hadn't died in the fall.

Before the coming of the horse, Indians used several methods of hunting bison. Sometimes, two hunters approached a herd from different directions. One wore a buffalo-calf robe, while the other was dressed in the pelt of a coyote or wolf. The hunter who masqueraded as a calf would make sounds like a calf in distress, which attracted the cows of the herd. When the bison got close enough, the hunters attacked with spears or arrows. In the wintertime, hunters donned snowshoes and

In this painting, George Catlin shows how hunters disguised themselves so they could sneak up on unsuspecting buffalo. NATIONAL MUSEUM OF AMERICAN ART, SMITHSONIAN INSTITUTION.

In wintertime, the Indians hunted on snowshoes, as painted here by George Catlin. NATIONAL MUSEUM OF AMERICAN ART, SMITHSONIAN INSTITUTION.

chased the animals into snowdrifts, where they could easily be killed.

The most efficient way to kill bison, however, was to take advantage of their herding instinct. One technique involved building a partially fenced area, called a surround or pound, into which the animals were driven. After being trapped in the surround, the buffalo were killed with spears and arrows.

An elderly Blackfeet named Weasel Tail told anthropologist John Ewers the stories he'd heard about how Blackfeet buffalo hunts were carried out in the old days. The travois that the dogs would pull were set up on end in a semicircle and tied together to make a fence downwind of the herd.

That way, the buffalo couldn't smell the women and dogs that hid behind the travois. (Children usually stayed behind at camp with the older women and men.) When everything was in place, two men would approach the buffalo from upwind, alarming them, and as the animals began to run, other men closed in from the sides, forcing the buffalo toward the barrier. Once the animals were trapped, the hunters attacked them.

Another method was used when the bison headed for protected wooded areas to spend the winter. Hunters cut down trees and built a three-sided corral at the base of a hill. They laid poles on the ground and smeared them with a mixture of manure and water, which created a slippery surface, making it difficult for the animals to escape.

Buffalo Jumps

The most effective way to hunt buffalo was to stampede a herd over a cliff, as Old Man taught the Blackfeet. Cliffs that were used over and over again are called "pishkins" or buffalo jumps.

The best known pishkin is located in Alberta, Canada, and is named Head-Smashed-In Buffalo Jump. The name doesn't describe what happened to the buffalo; instead, it honors one young Indian who fell over the cliff and died with a crushed skull. Archaeologists have studied this site and learned a great deal about how the animals were hunted and processed. This particular pishkin was used for thousands of years, from about 5,700 years ago until 200 years ago.

When buffalo ran over cliffs, like this one at Head-Smashed-In Buffalo Jump, they were killed or seriously injured.

A buffalo jump had four parts: the gathering basin, where the bison were first concentrated; the drive lanes, which directed the animals to the cliff; the cliff kill site, where the bodies of the bison landed; and the processing area, where the carcasses were butchered and various parts of the animal processed.

The gathering basin lay on the plain above the cliff, where there was plenty of fresh grass and water into the fall. Late fall was the perfect time for a big buffalo hunt. By then, the animals' winter coats had grown long and thick, which provided the people with warm buffalo robes. The animals were also fat and healthy after a summer of plenty to eat, and the cool weather helped keep the meat from spoiling as the Indians hurried to process the abundance of meat after the hunt.

Large numbers of Indians gathered to participate in the fall hunt and the processing of the carcasses. Everyone had a

The gathering basin at Ulm Pishkun State Park in Montana shows no sign of the deadly cliff nearby. DOROTHY H. PATENT

role to play in the drama. People probably stationed themselves along the thousands of piles of stones, called cairns, that made up the driving lanes. At Head-Smashed-In, the remains of rows of cairns still extend 8.75 miles (14 kilometers) from the cliff into the gathering basin. The cairns themselves might have served as markers, or they could have supported piles of brush. People may have crouched behind the brush and jumped up and yelled and waved their arms to keep the animals moving through the driving lanes.

As the people hid and waited, swift-running young men would lure the herd by bleating like lost buffalo calves. As the animals drew near the lanes, hunters would silently spread out behind them, then start yelling and waving to frighten the herd into running toward the cliff. The young men in front would quickly swing under the cliff edge into a small cave, and the buffalo would continue running right over the cliff to their death.

The cliff at Head-Smashed-In now stands about 30 feet (9 meters) above the ground. But at the base of the cliff are 36 feet (11 meters) of bison bones mixed with soil, so in prehistoric times, the animals must have fallen 60 feet (18 meters) or more.

When the first buffalo fell over a pishkin cliff, most of them probably died from their injuries. Many that followed may have been only injured, but hunters were ready to kill them with spears or arrows, or by smashing them in the head with stone mallets. Some tribes believed it was important to kill all the animals, not letting a single one escape to warn other bison what could happen to them in the future.

Buffalo are herd animals that stay together when alarmed.

Buffalo Meat

The Indians processed as many of the animals as they could. The tongues, a favorite delicacy, were eaten first. The humps and livers were also savored. The Indians ate the kidneys and intestines, and the blood was made into soup. The fall hunt provided an important source of food for the winter. Some of the meat was cut into strips and dried on wooden racks for later consumption. Because so much of the water evaporated as the strips dried, they weighed only about a sixth as much as raw meat, and they could last for three years. But the dried meat also could absorb water when the weather was humid—in which case, it rotted. Also, chewing the tough, dry strips was difficult.

Unique heavy stone mallets first show up in layers at Head-Smashed-In from about 6,000 years ago. Some archaeologists believe that that was when Indians first started making pemmican, a special food that provides excellent nutrition and that can last for several years. Pemmican was a great improvement over plain dried meat. It was easier to eat, more nutritious, and stayed edible for even longer. Pemmican recipes varied from tribe to tribe. The simplest form was called summer pemmican. The dried meat was pounded, using mallets, into a powder that was placed in buffalo rawhide bags. Then hot buffalo marrow fat was poured in. The heat of the fat killed bacteria or mold that might contaminate the meat, and the fat coated the bits of meat, preserving and protecting them. All the air was removed from the bag, which was then sealed. Summer pemmican could be stored for years.

To make another popular form of pemmican that was especially nutritious, the dried buffalo meat was pounded into a powder and mixed with dried berries as well as marrow fat. When meat and berries were abundant, lots of pemmican could be made, and the people were able to survive through hard times.

During World War II, many buffalo jump sites were destroyed. Bones contain a lot of phosphorus, which is used to make both explosives and fertilizer. The piles at the base of pishkins contained many tons of bones, which could be mined for the phosphorus. For example, 150 tons of bone meal were taken out at Ulm Pishkun Buffalo Jump in Montana. But Head-Smashed-In was located too far from any railroad and thus avoided this fate, so archaeologists have been

George Catlin painted these Sioux Indians processing buffalo meat.
NATIONAL MUSEUM OF AMERICAN ART, SMITHSONIAN INSTITUTION.

able to study it carefully and have learned a great deal about ancient buffalo jumps.

The processing area at Head-Smashed-In lies just below the foot of the cliff where the dead bison lay. Archaeologists have uncovered pits where cracked bones were boiled to yield grease. The pits were lined with hides and filled with water. Stones heated in a fire were dropped into the pits to bring the water to the boil. Four thousand tons of cracked boiling rocks littered the area, and more than 100,000 arrowheads were found. Since many buffalo died in the fall, and arrows were only one way that injured buffalo were killed, hundreds of thousands—perhaps millions—of buffalo died here over the years.

Using All of the Buffalo

The Indians used buffalo for more than food. Buffalo parts had more than a hundred uses. Hides were especially valuable. Hides from animals hunted in spring or summer, when the fur was short, were treated to become leather for making clothing, bags, saddles, and tepee coverings. It took from seven to twenty hides to cover a tepee. Several more were used inside as dividers between parts of the tepee, as decorations, and as bedding. Hides from animals killed in late fall or winter, when the fur was thicker, became robes for sleeping and for wearing over the shoulders during winter weather, as well as gloves and winter moccasins.

Buffalo hides had many uses. A hide with thick fur, like this one, would help keep someone warm in winter.

Preparing buffalo hides involved hard work that was usually done by the women. The hides were staked to the ground fur side down to hold them in place. Any flesh that clung to the hides had to be scraped off with a flint or metal tool, and the hide itself needed to be scraped down to an even thickness. For leather, the fur had to be removed. The resulting product was tough, strong rawhide, from which many useful items could be made, such as cradles, drum heads, boats, ropes, shields, and knife sheaths.

This Dakota Indian carrying case, called a parfleche, is made from rawhide. National Buffalo Museum.

Buffalo tails made good fly swatters. Dorothy H. Patent. Knife River Indian Villages National Historic Site.

If the hides were to be used for tepees or clothing, they were processed further. They were rubbed with a mixture of cooked buffalo brains, fat, and liver and then dried in the sun. Three more steps were required before the leather was soft and ready to use. For clothing, a fourth step—smoking the leather so it would remain soft even after a soaking rain—finally made it ready for sewing.

Buffalo tails had their own uses. They became effective fly swatters. They were also used in sweat lodges, special low huts built from willow branches and buffalo hides, for relaxing the muscles after a hunt and for purifying and healing ceremonies. Rocks were heated in a fire, and the Indians used buffalo tails to flick water onto the rocks to make steam.

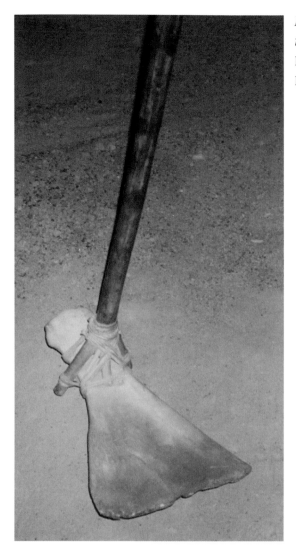

Buffalo shoulder blades were used to make garden hoes. DOROTHY H. PATENT. KNIFE RIVER INDIAN VILLAGES NATIONAL HISTORIC SITE.

Buffalo horns were fashioned into drinking cups, spoons, and ladles, while hooves became rattles. Chains of hooves joined by strips of leather were hung at the entrances to homes and used like doorbells. The hooves were also boiled to make glue.

The Indians found many ways to use buffalo bones and organs. Ribs were tied in a row to make a sled, and shoulder blades became gardening hoes. Bones formed the runners for dogsleds and could also be made into knife handles, pipes, war clubs, and other tools. The tendons that held bones together were fashioned into rope and thread. The internal organs also had their uses. Bison stomachs and bladders were cleaned and dried, then used to carry water.

Even buffalo dung was a valuable commodity. The dried patties, called buffalo chips, were gathered from the prairie and burned in campfires. Few trees grew on the prairies, so buffalo chips werc the only reliable source of fuel.

Chapter Three

SPIRITUAL RELATIONSHIP WITH THE BUFFALO

A Lakota Indian story tells how its people entered the world through a hole in the earth. One of them stayed behind, but all the rest were happy in the sunny, warm place, which provided everything they needed. Then things changed. Drought parched the land, and food became scarce. The people started dying of hunger. The one who had remained behind saw the people's suffering and decided to join them as a buffalo *(tatanka)*. The buffalo increased until they were abundant. Now the people had buffalo to hunt and eat, and they no longer starved. For this great gift, they honored the animal in their songs and dances and ceremonies.

Indians knew that they were just as much a part of the natural world as the plants and animals around them. They saw each kind of animal as another tribe similar to themselves, and they viewed animals as relatives sharing the Earth with them. As Oglala Sioux Chief Luther Standing Bear explained in his book, *Land of the Spotted Eagle,* "In the animal and bird world there existed a brotherly feeling that kept the Lakota, a tribal division of the Sioux, safe among them. And so close did some of the Lakotas come to their feathered and furred friends that in true brotherhood they spoke a common tongue."

The people understood that they depended on nature for survival, and they honored other living things. They believed that if they respected the animals they hunted, the animals would cooperate by giving themselves as food. The relationship went both ways. By giving themselves as food, the animals renewed themselves as well, in the form of new life that came into being in the springtime.

Vision Quests and Ceremonies

Among Plains tribes, vision quests were a vital part of growing up, especially for young men. To go on a vision quest meant venturing alone away from the village to fast and pray for an animal to come in a vision. If an animal did come, the young person would return to camp and consult a medicine man about the meaning of the vision. Often, the animal that appeared would become a "spirit animal" for that person, helping to guide him or her through difficult times of life.

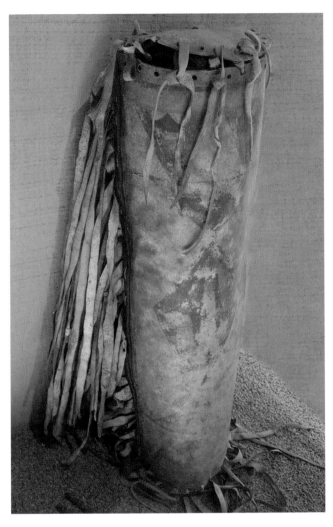

The medicine bundle played an important role in the lives of the Indians. When a person returned from a vision quest, a part of the body of the spirit animal, such as a tooth or a bit of fur, would be placed in a bundle along with other symbolic items such as crystals, seed pods, or tobacco. The medicine bundle held power for its owner. The bundles of medicine men would contain the herbs and other items that aided in healing, and sacred medicine bundles with great power belonged to the whole tribe.

Special ceremonies marked important events in the life of the tribe or its members, such as the naming of a child, a marriage, or preparing for a hunt. Medicine bundles were often a part of these ceremonies. A bundle might be hung from the fork of a sacred tree so the people could view it, for example.

Buffalo Power

In the relationship between humans and animals, the buffalo were especially important. As Oglala Sioux medicine man Black Elk expressed it, "The bison is the chief of all animals and represents the earth, the totality of all that is." Without the buffalo, tribes of the Plains could not survive. The lives of the tribes were tuned to the movements of the buffalo across the land, and the people honored the buffalo in many ways.

For most Plains tribes, an especially important event was the Sun Dance ceremony, which was held in early summer, at the beginning of the buffalo hunting season. Today, many tribes still carry out variations of this important ceremony. Buffalo are essential to the Sun Dance. A tree is cut down and placed at the center of a medicine lodge built especially for the ceremony. The details varied in the past, and still do, from tribe to tribe. Some tribes had a special hunt before the Sun Dance. The hunters brought back a buffalo head to place on the tree.

During the buffalo dance, the dancers imitated the actions of a buffalo pawing at the ground when angry or threatening. The custom in some tribes was for the men to try keeping their eyes fixed on the buffalo head. Dancers who maintained an unwavering gaze were awarded special buffalo tail sticks for beating on drums.

A specially painted buffalo skull was placed on an altar for the ceremony, and a feast of buffalo tongues, in which everyone got at least one taste, served to unite the people.

Buffalo skulls are an important part of ceremonies for Plains tribes.
Dorothy H. Patent. Fort Abraham Lincoln State Park Museum.

Buffalo Stones

The Plains Indians had a variety of ways of enticing the buffalo to them. The Blackfeet used a stone that looked something like a buffalo. Called an "iniskim" or buffalo rock, it had four bumps like the legs of a buffalo. There are many versions of the legend that explains how the iniskim came to the people, but the basic story is that in the long-ago time the tribe was starving in the winter, for the buffalo were not to be found. A humble woman went out to find firewood and heard singing. She looked around but could see no one. Then she realized that the singing was coming from the ground nearby. She looked down and saw a strange rock sitting on a

Buffalo stones like this one, made from lava rock and painted red, were used to call in the buffalo. DOROTHY H. PATENT. MUSEUM OF THE PLAINS INDIAN.

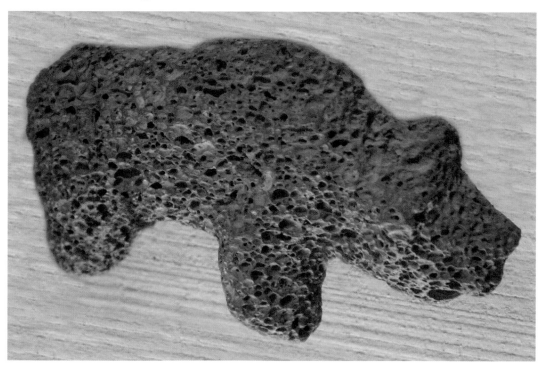

Many buffalo stones were individual sections of ammonite fossils that had fallen apart.

log, nestled among strands of buffalo hair. The rock sang out, "Take me, I am powerful."

The woman took the stone back to the camp and told her husband how she had found it. Other people who were in the tepee heard her story. The woman rubbed fat onto the rock, and it sang again. It told the people that it could bring the buffalo to them. Their arrival would be announced by a storm that passed through the camp, followed by a lone bull buffalo. The people were not to harm this lone bull.

Sure enough, a storm came that night, and so did the bull. The people left the bull alone, and in the morning a herd of buffalo grazed right next to the camp.

From then on, the iniskim was honored. Legend says that an iniskim would signal its presence by singing or chirping. When the Blackfeet found an iniskim, they painted it red and kept it in a medicine bundle wrapped in the hide of an unborn buffalo calf. It was then used in special ceremonies to call the buffalo.

The iniskim is indeed a special stone—it is often a fossil. Many millions of years ago, the Western Interior Seaway covered much of the land of the Blackfeet. Ancient relatives of squid that were similar to modern nautiluses lived in this sea. These animals, called ammonites, lived in spiral shells. As an ammonite grew, it walled off sections of its shell, which became filled with gas, which made the shell buoyant. Ammonite shells commonly became fossilized, and sometimes the separate sections of the shell came apart from one another. An iniskim is actually one section of an ammonite shell.

Mandan/Hidatsa Buffalo Dances

The Mandan and Hidatsa Indians lived in villages along the Missouri River in what is now North Dakota. These two tribes, each with different origins and quite different languages, came to live together, and they developed shared ceremonies. One of these was the Buffalo Bull Dance, performed by the men to bring buffalo closer to the village.

Karl Bodmer painted this Mandan buffalo dancer in the 1800s.
JOSLYN ART MUSEUM

The Dance of the White Buffalo Cow Society *was painted by Karl Bodmer.*
JOSLYN ART MUSEUM.

The dancers decorated their bodies with red, white, and black paint and wore buffalo-hair anklets and buffalo-hide masks. They stomped and bellowed like buffalo for hours. When a dancer tired and slumped to the ground, bystanders struck the fallen man with a blunt arrow, dragged him out of the circle, and pretended to skin him as they would a dead buffalo. A new dancer took his place, and the dancing continued until the buffalo were sighted.

Respected older women of these tribes belonged to the White Buffalo Cow Society. In winter, on the shortest day of the year, these women danced to help bring the buffalo so they could be hunted. They sometimes danced at other times as well, if the buffalo were hard to find. Their leader wore a rare white-buffalo robe. The dancers swayed from side to side to music played by male musicians. Everyone in the village knew to stay quiet during this important ceremony.

Chapter Four

THE ARRIVAL OF HORSES AND WHITE MEN

Long, long ago, an Arikara story says, the buffalo crashed into their villages, killing the people and devouring their bodies. After the buffalo left, the surviving people returned and placed what remained of the bodies on wooden scaffolds. A sixteen-year-old boy who had lost both his parents to the buffalo visited their scaffolds. He cried and cried until he fell asleep. He dreamed about two men, who told him the dead could come back to life and showed him how to make arrowheads and arrows. In the morning the boy went to the scaffolds and touched the bodies and told the dead people to wake up and get busy making weapons.

The men also said the animals would decide what would happen to the buffalo, so the elk, coyotes, bears, and all the others met. The horse complained that the buffalo were killing and eating humans instead of eating grass as they should. But a buffalo replied that it liked eating people, then suggested a race. "If I win, I will continue to eat humans. But if you beat me, you'll get your way." The horse agreed, and a strong buffalo bull and a powerful horse set up to race to the water's edge. The horse took the lead, so the humans mounted the horses and chased after the buffalo, shooting at them with their bows and arrows. The horse said it would keep helping the humans if the people agreed to take care of it. From then on, people could hunt buffalo on horseback.

The cultures of the Plains Indians are so tied to the horse in our minds that it is difficult to imagine their lives without them. Actually, very far in the past, horses did live in North America, but they became extinct about 10,000 years ago. The grasslands of the Plains were a natural home to horses, so they thrived there once they returned.

The Arrival of Horses

The Spanish brought horses to Mexico and then to southwestern North America in the 1500s. At first, Indians feared horses, for these unfamiliar animals gave the Spanish a great advantage in war. But the fear didn't last long.

Indians working on Spanish ranches in New Mexico

The horses brought to North America by the Spanish looked much like these present-day wild horses on the Pryor Mountain Wild Horse Range in Montana.

learned how to care for, ride, and train horses, and they passed their knowledge on to other Indians. We don't know exactly how fast the various tribes learned the value of using horses, but we do have some dates. In the 1650s, the Spanish traded horses to the Apaches in return for Wichita slaves, and by 1687 Indians in Texas were already hunting buffalo on horseback. Horses reached the Mandans on the Missouri River by 1739, and by 1754 the Gros Ventre Indians on the northern plains had already mastered horsemanship. All the Plains tribes seem to have had horses by 1770.

Adapting to Horses

The horse completely transformed Plains Indian culture. Horses moved much more quickly than dogs, and their greater size and strength meant more goods could be transported from place to place more quickly. A dog could drag only about 75 pounds on a travois and could travel only five or six miles a day. A horse could carry 200 pounds on its back, or 300 pounds on a travois, and cover twice as many miles in a day as a dog. Horses also provided great advantages in warfare and hunting. People could travel long distances much faster on horseback than they could on foot, and mounted hunters and warriors could attack more rapidly and forcefully.

With horses, the Indians could also make larger tepees. Before, tepees were made of seven or eight buffalo hides. But a horse could carry the weight of more than a dozen hides. An Indian band could cover much more distance with much less stress by riding on the backs of horses instead of trudging on foot across the prairies. The Indians became much more mobile, and some tribes that hadn't relied on buffalo previously moved into the Plains, since horses made buffalo hunting so much easier. White settlement in the east also put pressure on eastern tribes to move farther west.

New Ways to Hunt

The old methods of buffalo hunting were abandoned once a tribe had mastered horseback riding. A man riding a well-trained horse, called a buffalo runner, could easily kill three or four buffalo in a day, providing enough food for his family for several months. Learning how to hunt bison effectively wasn't easy for either the hunter or his horse, and a good buffalo runner was highly valued and pampered. To conserve the buffalo runner's strength, some hunters rode a different horse to the hunt, mounting his buffalo runner only when the chase began. Buffalo runners were sometimes taken into the tepee during the night for protection.

Everything became streamlined for a buffalo hunt. The men wore minimal clothing and often rode bareback. They used a rope looped around the horse's lower jaw instead of a

The buffalo hunt was a favorite subject of C.M. Russell's paintings.
AMON CARTER MUSEUM.

bridle to keep in touch with their mounts. As horse and rider approached the buffalo, the hunter would single out one animal to chase. The horse focused on that animal, needing no further guidance from the rider, who could concentrate on firing off arrows at just the right time. A bow with arrows was the best weapon, since a good hunter could shoot arrow after arrow. With the guns of those days, each shot had to be separately loaded, which wasn't easy atop a galloping horse. And loading took precious time.

A hunter on horseback could easily single out a buffalo to shoot from a grazing group like this one.

Broad arrow points made of bone, flint, or steel that would cause plenty of bleeding were favored. The perfect shot was one made just as the buffalo strode forward, which caused its ribs to separate. The arrow could then pass between the ribs and into the heart. A perfect shot downed the buffalo with a single arrow.

When the demand for buffalo skins by white traders increased during the 1800s, Indians found a market for their hunting skills. Some Indians began to hunt not just to supply meat and other buffalo products for their own families and tribes but also so they could trade with whites for guns and goods such as metal pots and pans or cloth. With the mobility provided by horses, hunting buffalo no longer required the cooperation of many people. A lone man could kill many buffalo by himself. One buffalo robe could be traded for a large kettle; four could bring a warm woolen Hudson Bay blanket. With eight robes, a hunter could acquire a rifle and a hundred rounds of ammunition.

Increased hunting by Indians probably had only a small effect on bison numbers. Indian populations on the prairies had already been devastated by the white man's diseases, especially smallpox, which decimated entire villages. But disease was only the first problem the whites brought to the Indians.

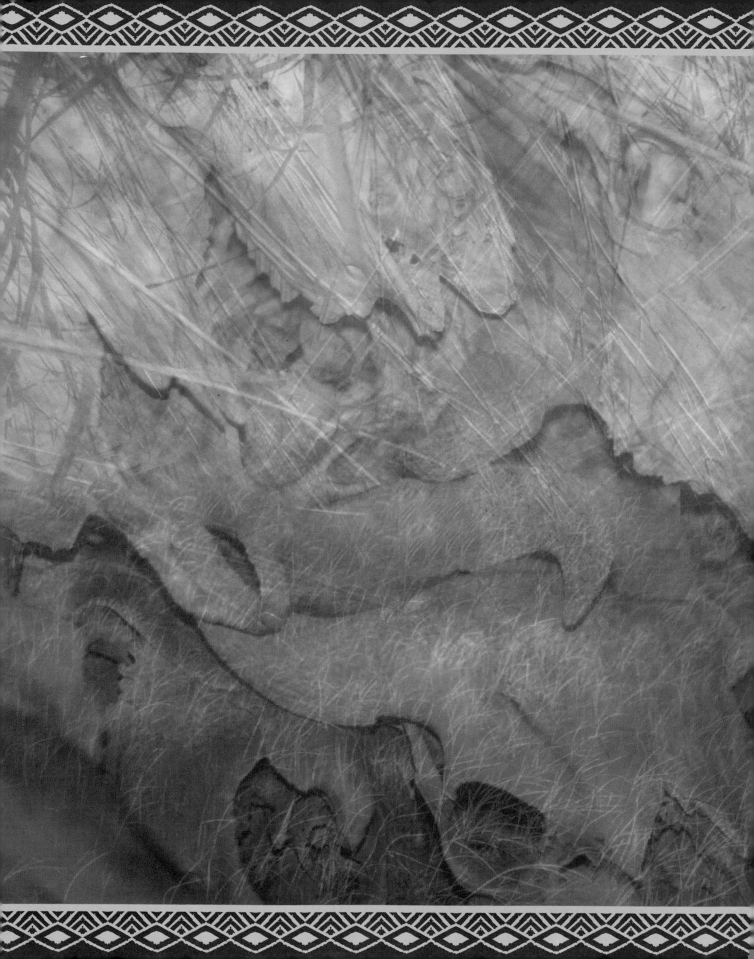

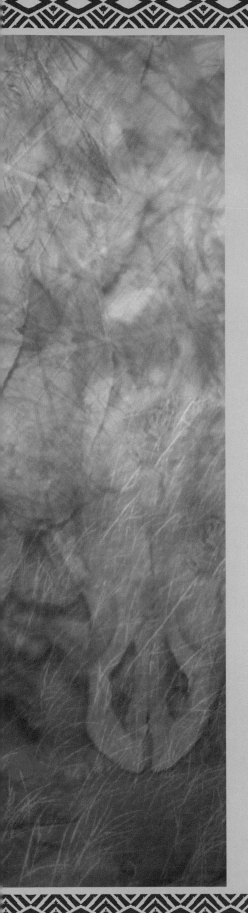

Chapter Five

DESTROYING THE WORLD OF THE BISON AND THE INDIANS

In the old days, the Kiowa say, the people loved the buffalo. They thanked and honored them well since they provided the people with their meat, hides, and other useful parts. In return, the buffalo loved and protected the people. When the white men came, the buffalo tried to protect their Indian friends by digging up the white man's gardens and tearing up his railroad tracks. But the white men sent soldiers with rifles, then hunters whose job it was just to kill the buffalo.

Finally, when they were almost all gone, the buffalo realized they could no longer protect the Indians. The few remnants of the great herds met to decide what to do. One morning, a young Indian woman got up early to fetch water. In the mist, she saw an old cow buffalo leading what remained of the buffalo—a few young cows and calves, along with the few surviving young bulls. The animals walked straight toward a big mountain, and the mountain opened up, revealing a beautiful land with clear waters and fresh green grass, the way it had been before the white men came. The buffalo entered the gap in the mountain, and it closed up behind them. They were never seen again.

In 1804, the Lewis and Clark expedition headed up the Missouri River to explore the unknown. Until then, the only white people who had entered the prairie region were Spanish explorers in the 1500s and British and French fur traders and trappers from what is now Canada in the 1700s. The United States had recently bought the land between the Mississippi River and the Rocky Mountains from France in the Louisiana Purchase. President Thomas Jefferson believed the future of the country lay to the west, and he wanted to know about the resources of that territory: the animals, plants, minerals, waterways—whatever might prove useful to the young country.

As the expedition worked its way west, the explorers wrote of the abundance of wildlife. Over and over they commented on the huge herds of bison in their journals. For example, William Clark wrote in 1806, "I ascended to the

Large herds of buffalo once roamed all across the North American prairies.

high country and from an eminence I had a view of a greater number of buffalo than I had ever seen before at one time. I must have seen near 20,000 of these animals feeding on this plain." We can never know how many bison lived on the prairies in those days, but most estimates put the number at around 50 million.

Moving West

When the Lewis and Clark expedition returned in 1806, the United States consisted of only seventeen states, all located east of the Mississippi River. The expedition helped stimulate a rush to the west by white fur trappers and settlers. As the nineteenth century progressed, more and more whites headed west. Starting in the 1840s, thousands followed the Oregon Trail, and the California gold rush in 1848 attracted still more. The end of the Civil War in 1865 sent many landless or dispossessed people westward. The pressure on the Plains Indians to get out of the way kept building.

As whites settled on Indian lands, conflicts between the two cultures increased. The United States government made treaties with the Indians, promising them land in trade for peace—but then broke the treaties when white settlers wanted the land. The Indians realized that they couldn't trust the whites, and they began to see them as the enemy who would take their land and destroy their way of life.

The whites, in turn, saw both the Indians and the buffalo as the enemy. Bison interfered with the growing herds of cattle and blocked the passage of trains along the new tracks that kept extending farther and farther west. From the point of view of the whites, the nomadic Indians who wandered at will across the prairies stood in the way of progress, which, for the whites, meant settling the land for farming and ranching and putting up fences.

Meanwhile, the demand for buffalo hides grew as trains and riverboats brought in more and more hunters and made transport of hides back east easier. People wanted buffalo robes, and the tough leather was ideal for making belts used in factory machinery. Buffalo hunters often slaughtered hundreds of animals at a time, harvesting only the hides and perhaps the tongues, which were considered to be a special delicacy, leaving the rest to rot on the prairies.

As hunting for hides put pressure on both the animals and the Indians, the Indians began to fight back in earnest, and the United States Army retaliated. In 1866, Cheyenne Chief

Artist Walter Lockhart painted Shooting Bison from a Union Pacific Train *in 1931.* KANSAS STATE HISTORICAL SOCIETY.

Roman Nose warned the army, saying, "We will not have the wagons which make a noise [trains] in the hunting grounds of the buffalo. If the palefaces come farther into our land, there will be scalps of your brethren in the wigwams of the Cheyenne. I have spoken."

Fighting between the two peoples increased, and the soldiers usually lost the battles. The Indians had many advantages. They were fighting for their lives and the survival of their culture. They knew every hill and gully of the countryside, and Indian boys grew up learning how to fight on horseback. The soldiers, on the other hand, weren't used to guerrilla-style battle. Many of them were poorly trained recent immigrants from Europe who had trouble even understanding orders from their superiors.

As the army suffered one humiliating defeat after another, the leaders realized there was only one way to destroy the Indians—take away their source of food. As long as buffalo roamed the prairies, the Indians could survive and fight.

Some white people, however, were concerned about the increasing slaughter. In 1874, the United States Congress passed a law to save the buffalo, but President Ulysses S. Grant wouldn't sign it. As a former army commander, he understood that the buffalo had to go if the Indians were to be defeated. The following year, the Texas legislature considered a bill aimed at saving the last remnants of buffalo in that state. General Philip Sheridan, commander of the United States Army in the Plains region, spoke to them about the buffalo hunters: "They are destroying the Indian's commissary, and it is a well-known fact that an army losing its base

Buffalo were hunted almost to extinction during the nineteenth century.

of supplies is placed at a great disadvantage. Send them powder and lead, if you will; for the sake of lasting peace, let them kill, skin, and sell until the buffaloes are exterminated. Then your prairies can be covered with speckled cattle and the festive cowboy, who follows the hunter as a second forerunner of an advanced civilization."

The legislators gave up on the idea of saving the buffalo.

The slaughter continued. As rifles improved in accuracy, the success of the buffalo hunters soared. The men bragged of their exploits. Buffalo Bill Cody wrote in 1888, "During my engagement as a hunter for the company [the Kansas Pacific Railroad]—a period of less than eighteen months—I killed

4,280 buffalos." The prairies became littered with acres of buffalo carcasses. In Canada, the government didn't have a direct policy of eliminating the buffalo, but the herds that the Indians depended upon often migrated across the border with the United States. So, between the intentional slaughter south of the border and their own hunting for economic gain, the Canadians lost most of their buffalo as well.

The slaughter of the buffalo left the prairie littered with bones,
which were later collected and processed for their mineral content.

By the end of the nineteenth century, wild buffalo had all but disappeared. Some survived in Canada, but in the United States only twenty-three wild bison survived, in Yellowstone National Park.

Fortunately, the few Yellowstone and Canadian bison weren't the only survivors. Thanks to some Americans who had begun rescuing buffalo in the 1870s, several hundred also survived on private farms and ranches.

The generals were right about the Indians' need for buffalo. Without these animals to hunt, they could not survive free on the prairies. The army subdued tribe after tribe and forced them to live on reservations. In an attempt to destroy Indian cultures, Indian children were taken from their parents and sent to government boarding schools where they were trained in the ways of the whites by being forbidden to speak their own languages and forced to speak English. They also had their hair cut in the white man's style and had to wear white man's clothing. The prairies now belonged to the whites, who quickly settled the land.

Saving the Remnants

With the goal of conquering the Indians achieved, some people began to lament the loss of the buffalo. Even some of those who had devoted their lives to destroying buffalo, such as Buffalo Bill Cody and General Philip Sheridan, now turned their efforts to protecting what few bison were left. Before this symbol of wild America was almost lost forever, a new spirit of conservation awakened in the United States.

On December 8, 1905, fourteen men, including zoologists, conservationists, and editors, met to organize the American Bison Society, dedicated to saving this great animal.

William Hornaday, chief taxidermist for the United States National Museum, became president of the society. Nineteen years earlier, he had led an expedition into Montana dedicated to collecting specimens for the museum. He and his men had managed to kill twenty-five animals. Hornaday commented, "I was delighted with our remarkably good fortune in securing such a prize, for, owing to the rapidity with which the large buffaloes are being found and killed off these days, I had not hoped to capture a really old individual. Nearly every adult bull we took carried old bullets in his body."

These buffalo in Yellowstone National Park are descended from the few survivors of the slaughter in the nineteenth century.

About 4,000 buffalo live in Yellowstone National Park today.
COURTESY OF JAMES B. ARMSTRONG

In 1907, Congress set aside money to establish a federal buffalo range in Oklahoma. It was initially stocked with fifteen buffalo. Another refuge, the National Bison Range in Montana, received thirty-four animals from a private herd in 1909. The rescue of the buffalo was under way.

Today, more than 200,000 bison roam the prairies once more, in national and state parks and wildlife refuges, and on Indian reservations and private ranches. Unfortunately, the rescue of the buffalo mixed the wood and plains bison together, so that the two subspecies are no longer distinct. But despite this loss and the reduced genetic diversity of today's bison, the future of this great animal seems secure.

Chapter Six

Living into the Present and the Future

Long ago, before the Indians had horses, two Lakota Sioux warriors were out hunting for buffalo. They looked for days but found nothing. After climbing a butte to search the landscape, they saw a miraculous sight: a beautiful young woman floating through the air toward them, dressed in a shimmering white buckskin dress decorated with sacred designs.

One of the young men reached out to touch her—but she was the sacred White Buffalo Calf Woman, not to be touched. A black cloud descended upon him, and when it left, all that remained were bones.

The other warrior knelt down to pray. The woman told him to go back to his village and tell the chief, Hollow Horn, that she would come in four days with important information.

On the fourth day, she arrived in the village, carrying a sacred bundle containing the gift of a special sacred pipe. She taught the people seven sacred ceremonies, including the Sun Dance.

Before she left, she made a prophesy that at some future time the birth of a white buffalo calf would signal her return, which would help bring harmony and balance back to the Indian people and to the world.

The story of White Buffalo Calf Woman comes in many versions, but the basic story is similar. For generations, the Sioux people have honored the ceremonies bestowed upon them by White Buffalo Calf Woman. The sacred pipe she gave has been passed down through the generations; today it is kept by Lakota Sioux Chief Arvol Looking Horse, nineteenth-generation keeper of the pipe.

When the Indians came across a white buffalo, they usually killed it. The fate of the hide varied from tribe to tribe. Some would hoist it high on a pole near the tepee of a medicine man and let it slowly decay. Others would use it to make the robe part of a medicine bundle, or divide it up into pieces that were then distributed among several bundles. The power of the Mandan White Buffalo Cow Society dance was based on the spiritual importance of the white buffalo.

Miracle was pure white when she was born. COURTESY OF DAVE AND VAL HEIDER.

White Buffalo Return

On August 20, 1994, a white buffalo calf was born on the farm of Dave and Val Heider in Janesville, Wisconsin. The Heiders are not Indians, but news of the calf's birth spread quickly among the Indian tribes. Arvol Looking Horse and other Sioux leaders visited the farm and decided that this, indeed, was a sacred white buffalo calf, the first to be born since 1933. The Heiders realized that they had a responsibility to the people and to their special young buffalo. They named her Miracle and opened their farm and their hearts to anyone who wanted to come to see her.

During Miracle's second week of life, Floyd Hand, chief

This albino buffalo lives on the grounds of the National Buffalo Museum.

medicine man of the Sioux Nation in Pine Ridge, South Dakota, phoned the Heiders. He predicted that Miracle's father, Marvin, would die. He said he could see a black blockage inside the bull that would kill him. Two days later, Marvin lay dead. An autopsy revealed two large black masses of blood from ulcers in his stomach.

Miracle was not an albino, an animal born without the pigment melanin, which colors hair, skin, and eyes black or brown. She had brown eyes and dark skin under her white coat. The story of White Buffalo Calf Woman suggests that a truly sacred buffalo calf would change color, for when she left the Indian village, in the direction of the setting sun,

White Buffalo Calf Woman rolled over four times, becoming first a black buffalo, then a brown one, then a red one, and finally a white one.

When Miracle was only a few months old, her coat began to darken. Some observers thought that she went through the color changes just like White Buffalo Calf Woman; others thought her color changes weren't so clearly defined.

Throughout Miracle's life, Indians from tribes across the country, as well as those from the Plains, came to visit her. They honored Miracle by leaving eagle feathers and other

As Miracle grew up, her coat took on a yellowish tone.
COURTESY OF DAVE AND VAL HEIDER.

Miracle as an adult buffalo.

treasured objects tied to the pasture fence. Indians weren't the only ones to come. People from around the world valued this rare, sacred animal enough to cross oceans to see her. Tens of thousand of people visited the farm, in the hope that Miracle signaled a time of growing strength and pride among Native Americans.

Many tribes besides the Sioux value the white buffalo, and each tribe has its own interpretation of its meaning. However, a common feature of these beliefs is a hope for a return of harmony among the world's people and harmony in the natural world. As Arvol Looking Horse said at World Peace and Prayer Day, June 21, 2003, Australia, "Mother Earth is not a resource but rather the source of life itself."

Miracle became ill and died on September 19, 2004. She was buried next to her father, Marvin. Three hundred people, including Floyd Hand and other Indian leaders, attended her funeral.

Miracle isn't the only white buffalo calf in recent years. There have been several others, including one born on August 7, 2001, at a farm in Vanderbilt, Michigan. Arvol Looking Horse named her Wahos'i, which means "Messenger." On September 26, 2001, Looking Horse sent these words to the world: "White Buffalo Calf Woman's spirit would make her presence known, a sign of great changes signifying the Crossroads. I never dreamed I would live to

People from all over the world left mementos and treasures to honor Miracle and what she represented. COURTESY OF DAVE AND VAL HEIDER.

witness this momentous time. Eight other white buffalo have since stood upon Mother Earth. White Buffalo Calf Woman's spirit has announced her message of support in this time of great danger, and she continues to announce the message in the birth of each White Buffalo—each one of them a Sign, each one a fulfillment of ancient Prophecy as well as a new Prophecy for our times."

Like Miracle, Wahos'i's coat changed color as she grew to adulthood. Her first winter coat was nearly black, then her new coat the following spring was red. Then she became yellow. Now she looks like any other bison, with a mostly dark brown coat.

Like Miracle, Wahos'i was born white and then changed color.
COURTESY OF BETH O'ROURKE.

Indians Strengthen Their Cultures

During the last few decades, many Indian tribes in North America have worked hard to encourage pride in their cultures and to strengthen their economies. An important part of this recovery has been bringing buffalo back to the people by reintroducing them into their natural habitat on the prairie, on Indian reservations. As Fred DuBray of the Cheyenne River Sioux said, "We recognize the bison is a symbol of our strength and unity, and that as we bring our herds back to health, we will also bring our people back to health."

Mr. DuBray is the executive director of the InterTribal Bison Cooperative (ITBC), an organization dedicated to helping tribes obtain surplus buffalo from the various national and state parks and wildlife refuges where they now live. It also helps tribes with funding and provides information on managing the buffalo and their habitat. Fifty-one tribes are members of the ITBC, and about 15,000 buffalo now live on tribal lands.

The largest reservation buffalo herd, more than 3,000 strong, lives on the Cheyenne River Sioux Reservation in South Dakota. Some excess animals are sold, and some meat is sold off the reservation. More important, buffalo meat is contributed to the tribe's schools and programs for the elderly, sold in the local grocery store at reduced prices, and donated for use at various tribal events such as powwows. Other bison parts, such as the bones, are cleaned and used for making crafts or for ceremonies.

Bringing back the buffalo can be complicated, however.

These young buffalo represent the future of the Blackfeet buffalo herd.

The Blackfeet tribe in Montana, for example, has a herd but is still figuring out how many bison it can afford to keep and where to keep them. Many people in the tribe are happy about the buffalo. As Jerry Lunak, agriculture director for the Blackfeet Nation, says, "Most people just want to see them. As long as the buffalo are here, things are okay." But in just two years, a buffalo eats more than its worth in dollars, so how does the tribe balance the value of the buffalo as a spiritual symbol with the costs of maintaining the herd?

The Blackfeet Nation has a small herd of young buffalo, which will grow over time. The animals are kept in a pasture near the tourist town of East Glacier, and Jerry Lunak would like to see the animals become a draw for tourists. He says, "We are proud and fortunate to have the buffalo with us. After many centuries the Blackfeet and the buffalo still co-exist; we are truly blessed." A visitors' center at the buffalo pasture could help educate travelers not only about buffalo but also about the Blackfeet people and their history, he believes. Everyone would benefit from this kind of educational opportunity.

The Three Affiliated Tribes (Mandan, Hidatsa, and Arikara)

Buffalo on the Three Affiliated Tribes reservation in North Dakota.

in North Dakota face similar problems with their bison herd. Their 15,000-acre Figure Four Ranch features a bison herd of 600 animals as well as an elk herd. There are cabins and bed-and-breakfast facilities for visitors. They also produce buffalo jerky for sale and hope to expand their market. The Three Affliiated Tribes bison herd is expected to support itself.

Prairie Restoration

At the same time that the Indians are reviving their land and culture, the government and conservation organizations are working to revive the prairie. Today, national and state parks dot the midwest, and a number of methods are being used to bring back original prairie plants and animals. Park and refuge managers burn the grass to stimulate growth of native plants and to keep trees from taking over, and they have brought back native prairie animals such as the buffalo and the black-footed ferret. When these parks have more buffalo than the land can support, the excess animals may be used to revive a buffalo herd on an Indian reservation. For example, Theodore Roosevelt National Park in North Dakota has provided bison to tribes such as the Mandan, Hidatsa, and Arikara Nation in North Dakota; the Cheyenne River Sioux Tribe in South Dakota; and the Modoc tribe in Oklahoma.

Artists and the Buffalo

Indian artists are also returning to their cultural roots through their honoring of the buffalo. Valentina LaPier, part

Valentina LaPier painted this buffalo, which she titled Iini Pikuni, *with symbols and images representing the culture of the Blackfeet tribe.*

Blackfeet and part Little Shell, spoke with me about the value of buffalo and tradition in her art. She began to feel a real connection to bison when she became an artist. When she first saw George Catlin's famous image of countless buffalo flowing down the hills, covering the prairie, she realized "how small you would feel with that coming to you and knowing your whole survival depended on that thunder." It made her deeply aware of the importance of the rhythms of the seasons, how the buffalo come and go depending on the time of year, how the people once depended on these powerful animals.

The Blackfeet tribe has three branches, each with its own traditional imagery, and LaPier wants to use all three in her art. A trademark of her work are little squiggles, sometimes in partial spirals. These are like the hair of the buffalo. In 2004, the C.M. Russell Museum in Great Falls, Montana, sponsored artists in painting images on three-quarter-sized buffalo statues. When she found out about the project, LaPier knew she had to paint one of those statues with traditional Blackfeet images.

In addition to the big job of painting the buffalo statue, LaPier includes buffalo in many of her paintings. She begins each day by asking, "What is my true art today?" Like many native artists, she feels an obligation to uphold the traditional images, but she also wants to bring these traditional ideas into the modern world.

Strengthening Traditions

Across North America, Indian tribes are reviving their cultural roots, creating written and visual art, teaching their languages to their children, and finding ways of reconnecting with the natural world. They are also establishing companies and schools to provide income and education for their people and are sharing their wisdom by working to educate other peoples about their traditions.

Through all their history, the Indians of the Plains have honored the buffalo, and they continue to do so today. The

buffalo, like the Indians, suffered greatly at the hands of the dominant white culture in the past, and the Indians, like the buffalo, are coming back into their power and working toward a healthy, sustainable future for themselves and for the natural environment in which they live.

To Learn More

I used many different resources in researching this book, including websites, books on Indian traditions and on buffalo, and museums in both the United States and Canada. I also had discussions with Native Americans and made visits to buffalo herds.

Since the information is so scattered, it's difficult to list books that might be useful to readers, but I can mention a few. *The Buffalo Book: The Full Saga of the American Animal* by David A. Dary, (Athens, Ohio: Ohio University Press, 1989) has a lot to say about buffalo up to recent times. *Buffalo Nation: History and Legend of the North American Bison* by Valerius Geist (Stillwater, Minn.: Voyageur Press, 1996) has a great deal of information about bison in prehistory as well as buffalo-human relationships.

Useful books for young readers include *Buffalo Hunt* by Russell Freedman (New York: Holiday House, 1988), which focuses on how Indians hunted buffalo and features many paintings of the hunt. *Buffalo Sunrise: The Story of a North American Giant* by Diane Swanson (San Francisco: Sierra Club Books for Children, 1996) has good information about the lives of buffalo and some on their relationship with Indians. Sneed Collard's *The Prairie Builders: Reconstructing America's Lost Grasslands* (Boston: Houghton Mifflin, 2005) tells of recent efforts to bring back the vanishing prairie.

Readers interested in Indian spirituality can read *The Spiritual Legacy of the American Indian* (New York: Crossroad, 1982) or *Animals of the Soul: Sacred Animals of the Oglala Sioux* (Rockport, Mass.: Element, 1997), both by Joseph Epes Brown. A favorite book of mine, for all readers, is *Seeing the White Buffalo* by Robert Pickering (Boulder, Colo.: Denver Museum of Natural History Press, 1997), which discusses the white buffalo from the viewpoints of biology, the history and culture of American Indians, and the Heider family (on whose farm the white buffalo calf named Miracle was born), and also from a spiritual perspective.

Websites about buffalo abound, and they change quickly, so if you surf the web using key words related to your special interest, you are sure to come up with some good sites. For starters, try:

www.head-smashed-in.com for excellent information about how Indians hunted buffalo before they had horses.

http://www.psyeta.org/sa/sa1.1/lawrence.html has detailed information about the importance of buffalo to the Sun Dance.

To learn more about Miracle, go to:

www.homestead.com/whitebuffalomiracle. This site has many useful links.

I based my versions of the Indian stories that open the chapters on stories in different books.

CHAPTER ONE: From *Myths and Legends of the Great Plains* by Katharine Berry Judson (Chicago: McClurg, 1913).

CHAPTER TWO: From *Blackfoot Lodge Tales: The Story of a Prairie People* by George Bird Grinnell (Lincoln, Neb.: University of Nebraska Press, 1962).

CHAPTER THREE: From *The Lakota Way: Stories and Lessons for Living* by John M. Marshall III, ed. (New York: Viking Compass, 2001). The quotation from Black Elk on page 34 is from *Animals of the Soul: Sacred Animals of the Oglala Sioux* by Joseph Epes Brown (Rockport, Mass.: Element, 1997).

CHAPTER FOUR: From *Myths and Traditions of the Arikara Indians* by Douglas R. Parks, ed. (Lincoln, Neb.: University of Nebraska Press, 1996).

CHAPTER FIVE: From two sources: *American Indian Myths and Legends* by Richard Erdoes and Alfonso Ortiz, eds. (New York: Pantheon Books, 1984), and *Keepers of the Animals: Native American Stories and Wildlife Activities for Children* by Michael J. Caduto and Joseph Bruchac (Golden, Colo.: Fulcrum Publishing, 1991).

CHAPTER SIX: Story from numerous sources.

The quotation from Chief Arvol Looking Horse on page 68 is from his book *White Buffalo Teachings* (Dreamkeepers Press, 2001).

INDEX

Note: Page numbers in **bold** type indicate photographs.